Table of Contents

1. Introduction

During the past year, the Consumer Financial Protection Bureau (CFPB) has engaged in an in-depth review of short-term small dollar loans, specifically payday loans extended by non-depository institutions and deposit advance products offered by a small, but growing, number of depository institutions to their deposit account customers. This review began with a field hearing held in Birmingham, Alabama in January 2012. At that event, CFPB Director Richard Cordray noted that "the purpose of th[e] field hearing, and the purpose of all our research and analysis and outreach on these issues, is to help us figure out how to determine the right approach to protect consumers and ensure that they have access to a small loan market that is fair, transparent, and competitive." Director Cordray went on to state that "[t]hrough forums like this and through our supervision program, we will systematically gather data to get a complete picture of the payday market and its impact on consumers," including how consumers "are affected by long-term use of these products."[1]

Both at the field hearing and in response to a subsequent request for information, the CFPB heard from consumers who use these products.[2] On one hand, some consumers provided favorable responses about the speed at which these loans are given, the availability of these loans for some consumers who may not qualify for other credit products, and consumers' ability to use these loans as a way to avoid overdrawing a deposit account or paying a bill late. On the other hand, consumers raised concerns such as the risk of being unable to repay the loan while still having enough money left over for other expenses, the high cost of the loan, and aggressive debt collection practices in the case of delinquency or default.

These discussions and submissions underscore the importance of undertaking a data-driven analysis of the use of these products and the longer-term outcomes that borrowers experience. Because Congress authorized the CFPB to supervise both depository and non-depository institutions, over the past year we have been able to obtain data from a number of market

---

[1] The full transcript of Director Cordray's speech is available at http://www.consumerfinance.gov/speeches/remarks-by-richard-cordray-at-the-payday-loan-field-hearing-in-birmingham-al/.

[2] Comments received in response to this request for information are available for review at http://www.regulations.gov/#!searchResults;rpp=25;po=0;s=cfpb-2012-0009.

participants that offer either deposit advance products or payday loans. At the same time, the CFPB has been conducting an in-depth review of overdraft products and practices, which some consumers may also use to meet financial shortfalls. The CFPB plans to issue a preliminary report based on the results of that study shortly.

This white paper summarizes the initial findings of the CFPB's analysis of payday loans and deposit advances. It describes the features of typical payday loan and deposit advance products. The paper then presents initial findings using supervisory data the CFPB has obtained from a number of institutions that provide these products.[3] The analysis reported here reflects considerations needed to preserve the confidentiality of the institutions that provided the information used in this paper.

The CFPB has a statutory obligation to promote markets that are fair, transparent, and competitive. Consequently, this white paper has two primary purposes. First, we seek to provide information that may facilitate discussion of policy issues around a shared set of facts. Second, we seek to provide market participants with a clear statement of the concerns our analysis raises.

The CFPB recognizes that demand exists for small dollar credit products. These types of credit products can be helpful for consumers if they are structured to facilitate successful repayment without the need to repeatedly borrow at a high cost. However, if the cost and structure of a particular loan make it difficult for the consumer to repay, this type of product may further impair the consumer's finances. A primary focus is on what we term "sustained use"—the long-term use of a short-term high-cost product evidenced by a pattern of repeatedly rolling over or consistently re-borrowing, resulting in the consumer incurring a high level of accumulated fees.[4]

---

[3] The CFPB considers all supervisory information to be confidential. Consistent with CFPB's rules, the data findings presented in the white paper do not directly or indirectly identify the institutions or consumers involved. See CFPB's final rule on the *Disclosure of Records and Information,* 12 C.F.R. § 1070.41(c).

[4] For purposes of this white paper, sustained use is not measured only by the number of loans that are taken by a consumer over a certain period of time, but the extent to which loans are taken on a consecutive or largely uninterrupted basis. For example, one consumer who takes out six loans in a year may do so on a sporadic basis, paying back each loan when due, and taking significant breaks between each use. Another consumer might also have taken out six loans, but sequentially with little or no break between periods of indebtedness. The latter scenario would be more indicative of sustained use than the former.

The findings reported in this white paper indicate that these risks exist for a sizable segment of consumers who use these products.

2. Overview of Payday Loans and Deposit Advances

Given the general similarities in structure, purpose, and the consumer protection concerns these products raise, this paper provides a parallel analysis of payday loans and deposit advances.[5]

Payday loans offered by non-depository institutions and deposit advances offered by certain depository institutions are generally marketed as a way to bridge unexpected financial short-falls between paychecks, receipt of benefits, or other sources of income. The products provide ready access to funds for a short period of time with very limited underwriting. Rather than charging a periodic interest rate which would generate a dollar cost that depends on the amount of time the debt is outstanding, payday and deposit advance lenders charge a set fee that is based upon the amount borrowed and does not vary with loan duration. [6]

Payday loans are typically structured with a single balloon payment of the amount borrowed and fees, timed to coincide with the borrower's next payday or other receipt of income. Loans are repaid at the storefront or—in the event the borrower does not return to the storefront—repayment may be initiated by the lender by presenting the consumer's personal check or effecting a pre-authorized electronic debit of the consumer's deposit account.[7]

Deposit advances are offered by a small number of depository institutions to certain deposit account holders who have recurring electronic deposits, such as a direct deposit of their

---

[5] The descriptions of payday loans and deposit advances provided in this section reflect market research and do not imply that the CFPB has necessarily approved or critiqued any particular aspects of the features or operation of these products from a regulatory or supervisory standpoint.

[6] Some states have minimum loan durations as part of their payday lending laws. Depository institutions offering deposit advances may have internal policies that affect the minimum amount of time an advance is outstanding.

[7] Originally offered only by storefront lenders, these loans are now increasingly offered online. Online payday loans are discussed in more depth at the end of Section 2.1 on payday loans, but are not the focus of this white paper.

paycheck, to their accounts.[8] Like payday loans, deposit advances are typically structured as short-term loans. However, deposit advances do not have a predetermined repayment date. Instead, deposit advance agreements typically stipulate that repayment will automatically be taken out of the borrower's next qualifying electronic deposit. Deposit advances are typically requested through online banking or over the phone, although at some institutions they may be requested at a branch.

Despite the general similarities between payday loans and deposit advances, particularly in the consumer protection issues they raise, there are significant differences in delivery costs and credit risk as those products are typically structured today.

Available data indicate that storefront payday lenders have significant fixed costs associated with customer acquisition and with the operation of retail storefront locations.[9] Although storefront lenders generally require borrowers to provide a personal check or debit authorization, both the credit extensions and loan repayments typically take place at the storefront. There is less available information regarding the costs of offering a deposit advance product. However, the product is offered only to existing customers and is an automated feature of a deposit account, akin to linking a deposit account to a line of credit.

Payday lending also involves somewhat greater credit risk than a deposit advance. The payday lender is dependent upon information it can obtain from the borrower or from external sources to assess the borrower's likelihood of repayment. With deposit advance, the depository institution has insight into the customer's flow of funds over a period of time before extending eligibility to the customer. Furthermore, similar to standard overdraft coverage, depository institutions can immediately debit incoming funds (certain electronic deposits in the case of deposit advances) to obtain the repayment of an advance, before paying other transactions that occur on the same day. Payday industry data indicate loss rates of around 5% of loan

---

[8] We use the term "depository institution" throughout this white paper to generally refer to both banks and credit unions. "Deposit account" refers to checking accounts offered by a bank and share draft accounts offered by a credit union.

[9] For a more detailed discussion of storefront payday economics, see Flannery, Mark, and Katherine Samolyk, *Scale Economies at Payday Loan Stores*, Proceedings of the Federal Reserve Bank of Chicago's 43rd Annual Conference on Bank Structure and Competition (May 17, 2007).

originations for large storefront lenders.[10] Initial analysis of loan charge-off rates on deposit advances conducted by the CPFB in connection with this study suggests that deposit advance loss rates are lower than those reported for storefront payday loans.

The features and operation of these two products are discussed separately in more detail below.

2.1 Payday Loans

As just explained, a payday loan is typically structured as a closed-end single payment loan with a due date that coincides with the borrower's next payday or receipt of other income. Because the due date is timed in this manner, the loan term is typically two weeks. However, the term could be shorter for consumers who are paid on a weekly basis or longer for those receiving income once a month. Variants of this model exist, including open-end lines of credit and longer-term loans (which may be repayable in installments). The structure of these variations may be driven by state law or other factors.

A consumer obtaining a payday loan at a storefront location must either provide a personal check to the lender or an authorization to electronically debit her deposit account for the loan amount and associated fee. Although the check or authorization essentially serves as a form of security for the loan, the borrower usually agrees to return to the storefront when the loan is due to make repayment in person. If the consumer does not return to the storefront when the loan is due, a lender has the option of depositing the consumer's check or initiating an electronic withdrawal from the consumer's deposit account.

Cost. The cost of a payday loan is a fee which is typically based on the amount advanced, and does not vary with the duration of the loan. The cost is usually expressed as a dollar fee per $100 borrowed. Fees at storefront payday lenders generally range from $10 to $20 per $100, though loans with higher fees are possible. Variations often reflect differences in state laws setting

---

[10] For example, one payday trade association notes that "[n]inety five percent of loans are repaid when due..." See Community Financial Services Association of America, *Myth v. Reality*, available at http://cfsaa.com/aboutthepaydayindustry/myth-vs-reality.aspx.

maximum allowable fees. A fee of $15 per $100 is quite common for a storefront payday loan, and would yield an APR of 391% on a typical 14-day loan.

Eligibility. Many states set a limit on payday loan size; for example, $500 is a common loan limit. In order for a consumer to obtain a payday loan, a lender generally requires the consumer to present identification and documentation of income, and have a personal deposit account. Lenders generally do not consider a consumer's other financial obligations or credit score when determining eligibility; however, some lenders use specialty credit reporting firms to check for previous defaults on payday loans and perform other due diligence such as identity and deposit account verification. No collateral (other than the check or electronic debit authorization) is held for the loan.

Repayment. Storefront payday loan contracts generally require borrowers to return to the storefront to pay the loan and associated fee by the due date. If a borrower is unable to repay the full amount, the lender may give her the option to roll over the loan balance by paying a fee, usually equal to the original finance charge, in order to extend the loan until her next payday. If the lender is unwilling or—because of restrictions in state law—unable to directly roll over a loan, the borrower may instead repay the full amount due and then quickly take out a new loan.

Limits on Sustained Use. Historically, payday lending has been largely governed by state law, often through specific legislation that modifies a state usury law in order to permit payday lending. Hence, payday lenders are required to comply with varying laws in each state in which they are located. In states in which payday lending is permitted, laws often include provisions that attempt to limit sustained use, such as: (1) restrictions on the number of times a loan can be rolled over, (2) requirements to offer extended payment plans, (3) cooling-off periods between loans that are triggered after a period of time indebted or number of transactions conducted, (4) limits on loan size based on monthly income, and (5) limits on the number of loans that can be taken over a certain period of time. Individual lenders and trade associations may also adopt their own policies and best practices.[11]

---

[11] For example, one trade association whose membership includes storefront payday lenders, the Community Financial Services Association (CFSA), has adopted a set of best practices that include limits on roll overs and the availability of an extended payment plan. See *CFSA Member Best Practices*, available at http://cfsaa.com/cfsa-member-best-practices.aspx. Another trade association that also serves storefront payday lenders, the Financial Service Centers of America (FISCA), has adopted a similar code of conduct for extending credit. See *FISCA Code of*

Online Payday Lending

While not the subject of the findings of this white paper, the CFPB is separately analyzing the use of online payday loans. Online payday loans still make up a minority of the total loan volume; however, the online channel is steadily growing and some industry analysts believe it may eventually overtake storefront loan volume.[12] Variations on the loan structure, such as online payday installment loans and open-end lines of credit, are becoming more common.

In the online lending model, a consumer completes a loan application online and provides an authorization for the lender to electronically debit her deposit account. Other payment methods such as remotely-created checks or wire transfers may also be used. The loan proceeds are then deposited electronically into the consumer's deposit account. On the due date, the lender submits the debit authorization to the consumer's depository institution for repayment. Alternatively, the loan might be structured to provide for an automatic roll over, in which event the lender will submit a debit authorization for the fee only. If an online loan is set up to roll over automatically, the borrower must proactively contact the lender a few days before the electronic withdrawal is to occur to indicate that they wish to pay off the loan in full.

Online loans tend to be offered with fees equal to or higher than storefront loans. According to two industry reports, some of the key cost drivers for online payday lending are the cost of customer acquisition, often done by purchasing leads from lead generators, and loss rates which are reportedly higher for online loans than for storefront payday lending.[13]

Conduct in Offering Access to Credit, available at
http://www.fisca.org/Content/NavigationMenu/AboutFISCA/CodesofConduct/FiSCAPDACodesofConduct/default.htm.

[12] For example, some payday lending industry reports contain discussions of growth trends and loan volume projections. See, e.g., Stephens Inc. *Payday Loan Industry Report* (June 6, 2011) and JMP Securities' *Consumer Finance: Online Financial Services for the Underbanked* (Jan. 9, 2012).

[13] Cost drivers for the online payday lending industry are also discussed in the Stephens Inc. and JMP Securities reports, referenced in n. 12.

2.2 Deposit Advances

Deposit advances are lines of credit offered by depository institutions as a feature of an existing account. The product is available only to those consumers that receive electronic deposits on a recurring basis. Some institutions provide eligible consumers the option to sign up for this product; at other institutions, the feature is automatically provided to eligible consumers. When an advance is requested, funds are typically deposited into the consumer's account as soon as the advance is processed, subject to certain limitations on availability for use. Because advances will be repaid automatically when the next qualifying electronic deposits are made to the consumer's account, there is no fixed repayment date at the time the advance is taken. In the event an outstanding advance is not fully repaid by incoming electronic deposits within 35 days, the consumer's account will be debited for the amount due, even if this results in the associated deposit account being overdrawn.

Cost. Like payday loans, the fees associated with deposit advances typically do not vary with the time that the consumer has an outstanding loan balance. The fees are typically disclosed to consumers in terms of dollars per amount advanced. For example, the cost may be described as $2 in fees for every $20 borrowed, the equivalent of $10 per $100. Unlike a payday loan however, the repayment date is not set at the time of the advance and will vary depending on timing and amount of electronic deposits. Hence the fee cannot be used to calculate an APR for the advance at the time the credit is extended.

Eligibility and Credit Limit. A consumer is eligible for a deposit advance if she has a deposit account in good standing which has been open for a specified period and has a history of recurring electronic deposits above a minimum size. Individual depository institutions may impose additional eligibility criteria. Accounts can become ineligible for additional deposit advances for a number of reasons, such as a lack of sufficient recent electronic deposits or excessive overdrafts and non-sufficient funds (NSF) transactions.

Credit limits on the deposit advance product are generally set as a percentage of the account's monthly electronic deposits, up to a certain limit. For example, some depository institutions permit the deposit advance to be the lesser of $500 or 50% of the direct deposits from the preceding statement cycle. The advance limit does not include any associated fees that may be charged for the advance.

The depository institution relies on past electronic deposit history to anticipate the level of deposits that will likely be available as the source of repayment. It typically does not consider the consumer's overall outstanding debt service burden and living expenses. Like payday loans, traditional credit criteria are not used to determine eligibility.

Depository institutions that offer this product generally notify account holders that they are eligible to take advances through online alerts. An eligible consumer can initiate an advance online, via automated voice-assisted phone services, or—at some institutions—in person at a branch.

Repayment. Typically, repayment of an outstanding deposit advance balance is automatically debited from the consumer's account upon receipt of the next incoming qualifying electronic deposit. Qualifying electronic deposits used to repay advances can include recurring deposits (such as salary or government assistance or benefits) as well as one-time payments (such as a tax refund or expense reimbursement from an employer).

Generally, the depository institution captures repayment of advances and fees from the incoming electronic deposit before the consumer can use those funds for other expenses. If that electronic deposit is less than the outstanding deposit advance balance, institutions will typically collect the remaining balance from subsequent electronic deposits.

If an advance and the associated fee are not completely repaid through subsequent electronic deposits within 35 days, the depository institution may execute a forced repayment from the consumer's deposit account for the amount due, even if this causes the account to become overdrawn.

As with payday loans, there are variations of the typical deposit advance product. Some allow consumers to repay the loan through a series of installments over a period longer than 35 days. These repayment options may carry additional costs and restrictions.

Limits on Sustained Use. State-chartered depository institutions operate subject to state law, but, as currently structured, the deposit advance product does not meet the definition of payday lending contained in most state laws, and federally chartered institutions are not generally subject to such legislation. Consequently, it appears that depository institutions typically do not consider such laws in setting the features of deposit advance products. Most programs set limits on the number of consecutive months a consumer can use deposit advances. However, the amount of borrowing needed to trigger a cooling-off period or other mechanism to limit use varies across institutions.

Interplay with Overdraft. Because deposit advance and overdraft are both services tied to a deposit account, there is potential for various interactions between these products. Depository institutions frequently consider a consumer's overdraft and NSF activity when assessing continued eligibility for deposit advance.

If account balances are depleted, consumers may use a deposit advance to cover debits before those transactions are posted and thereby avoid incurring overdraft fees. However, if a consumer's account is already overdrawn when she takes a deposit advance, the advance proceeds are automatically applied to pay off the negative balance resulting from the overdraft and any associated fee first, with the remainder available for her use. In addition, a consumer's account may become overdrawn from a forced repayment on day 35 if there are insufficient funds in the account to cover the repayment. If this insufficient fund situation occurs, a consumer may be charged overdraft or NSF fees on subsequent items presented to the account.

3. Initial Data Findings

The CFPB's avenues of inquiry related to the use of payday loans and deposit advances include loan and borrower characteristics, usage patterns, and outcomes that are correlated with certain patterns of use. While our data do not represent all consumers using these products, our findings are an accurate representation of how these products are used by a sizable share of borrowers in the marketplace.

The following discussion provides initial data findings on consumer usage of storefront payday loans[14] and deposit advances.

3.1 Payday Loans

For our study of payday loans, we obtained data from a number of payday lenders to create a dataset of all payday loans extended by each lender for a minimum 12-month period. Information in the data allows us to identify the loans that were made to the same consumer at a given lender, but not to the same consumer across lenders. [15]

Our findings are derived from a subset of consumers in the full dataset. The sample consists of consumers who have a loan in our dataset in the first month of a 12-month period and then tracks usage across this timeframe. We limit our analysis to this subset of consumers because one focus of our analysis is sustained use, and consumers that we initially observe later in the data can only be followed for a more limited time. The start and end dates of lenders' 12-month

---

[14] As noted before, while the analysis in this white paper does not include any online payday loan usage, we plan to conduct a similar analysis of that market.

[15] Our sample consists of all loan activity conducted by an individual consumer at a given lender during the 12-month time period. A borrower may obtain loans from more than one payday lender; however, this analysis does not control for such cross-lender activity and thus potentially underestimates per-consumer usage. The impacts of cross-lender borrowing may be evaluated in subsequent empirical work. In addition, because we are analyzing results for individuals rather than households, we cannot determine whether other household members are using payday loans or have other relevant income that is not observed.

data reporting varies, which mitigates concerns about seasonality effects. Overall, the study sample consists of a total of approximately 15 million loans generated by storefronts in 33 states.[16]

3.1.1 Loan Characteristics

The median amount borrowed by consumers in our sample was $350. Loan amounts are often limited by state law, with a common maximum loan size of $500, though some states have lower or higher limits. Individual lender credit models may also influence loan amounts offered. The mean loan size was $392, signaling that there are more consumers with loan sizes substantially above the median than substantially below. Most loans in our sample cluster around $250, $300, and $500.

The payday loans we analyzed were single payment loans with a repayment scheduled to occur on the borrower's payday (or when they are scheduled to receive other regular sources of income). We found a median loan term of 14 days, and a mean loan term of 18.3 days.[17]

While payday loans are generally characterized as two-week loans, and we observed a significant number of loans with a 14-day loan duration, there are several explanations for the longer mean loan duration. One reason is state law, which can dictate minimum loan terms and other features.[18] In addition, loan due dates are impacted by the frequency at which consumers receive income, since due dates are generally set to align with a borrower's payday. We have data for a subset of our sample on the frequency with which consumers received income, which is illustrated in Figure 1 below. While over half of the consumers we observed were paid twice per

---

[16] Our sample does not include loans structured at origination to be repayable in installments over a longer period of time, such as those offered in Colorado. Colorado requires a minimum six month loan term. See Colorado Deferred Deposit Loan Act, 5-3.1-103.

[17] Loan duration is defined as the contractual duration when available. When contract duration is unavailable, duration is based on the date the loan was repaid. Average duration changes very little if loans for which contractual duration is unavailable are dropped from the sample.

[18] For example, if a consumer who is paid every two weeks takes out a payday loan three days before her next payday in a state with a minimum seven day loan term, her loan would not come due at that time. Rather, it would be scheduled for a subsequent payday, perhaps 17 days later.

month (thus receiving 24 paychecks per year if paid semi-monthly or 26 paychecks if paid bi-weekly), one-third of consumers were paid monthly.

Figure 1: Pay frequency reported at application

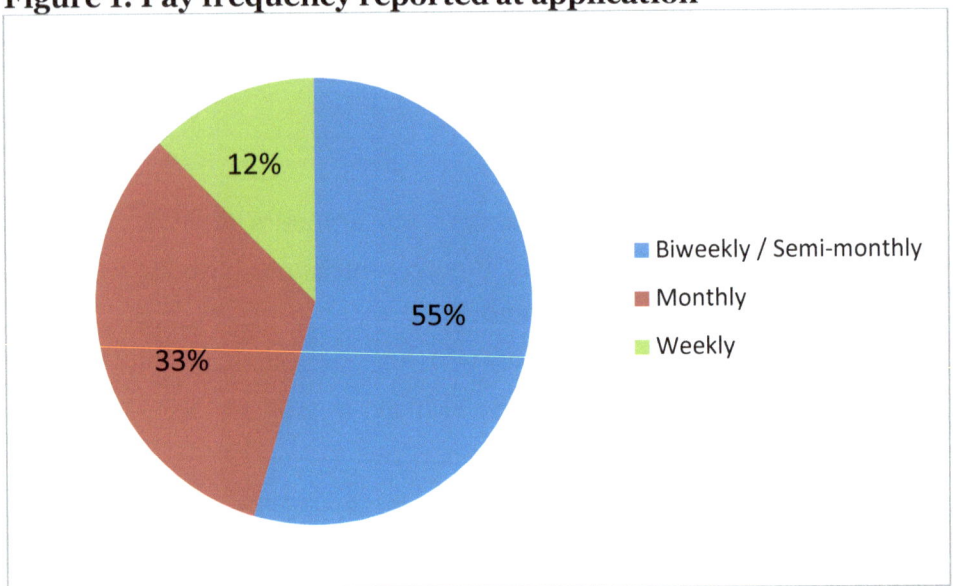

Most states with payday lending storefronts set a maximum fee per $100 borrowed that lenders may charge, which typically ranges between $10-20 per $100. A few states have higher or no limits, while others employ a sliding scale, depending on loan size.[19] The median fee we observed in our sample was $15 per $100. Table 1 provides a summary of mean and median loan amounts, fees per $100, duration, and APR for the loans in our sample.

---

[19] An example of a state with a sliding scale fee schedule is Michigan, where a fee of $15 is assessed on the first $100 borrowed, then $14 on the second $100, $13 on the third $100, and so on. See Michigan Deferred Presentment Service Transaction Act § 487.2153.

Table 1: Summary of loan characteristics

	Mean	Median
Loan amount	$392	$350
Fee per $100	$14.40	$15
Duration	18.3 days	14 days
APR	339%	322%

Note: Summary statistics should not be interpreted as reflective of the characteristics of an "average" loan. Individual data findings for average loan amount, fee, duration, and APR are calculated separately and do not relate to one another. For instance, the loans in our sample have a median cost of $15 per $100. This would equate to a fee of $52.50 on the median $350 loan. In this example, the borrower would owe $402.50 to be repaid on her due date. The APR on that particular loan with a median duration of 14 days would be 391%.

3.1.2 Borrower Income

Here, we examine the income that consumers document as part of the application process in order to qualify for a loan, and the source of that income.[20] Storefront payday borrowers in our sample have income that is largely concentrated in income categories ranging from $10,000-$40,000 on an annualized basis.[21]

---

[20] Consumers typically provide a recent pay stub, recent deposit account statement, or other information to document income as part of the application process.

[21] Our dataset includes information on the amount and frequency of income that can be used to calculate an annualized figure for each borrower in our sample. Because the source of this income information could be a paystub or deposit account statement, it may be net income after taxes and other items have been deducted. The income data reported in this section is only available for a sub-set of lenders in our sample.

Figure 2: Distribution of income reported at application

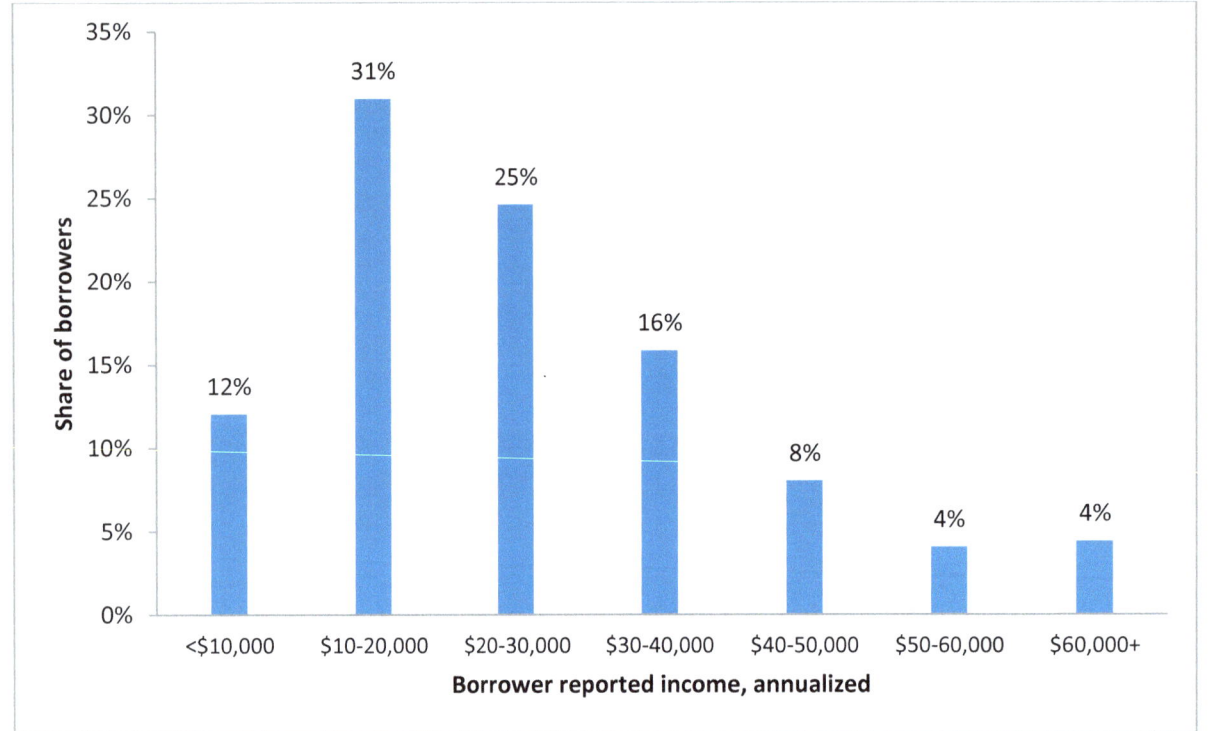

Note: Annualized income based on pay period amount and pay frequency reported at the time of payday application.

The median income is $22,476, although a quarter of borrowers have income of $33,876 or more.

Table 2: Borrower income reported at application

Mean	$26,167
25th percentile	$14,172
Median	$22,476
75th percentile	$33,876

It is important to note that income used in this analysis may not reflect total household income. Other income may be present in the household if the borrower receives income from more than one source or another person in the household also has an income source.

We also observed the source of this income. Three-quarters of consumers in our sample were employed either part- or full-time. A significant share of consumers—nearly 1 in 4—reported either some form of public assistance or other benefits (18%) or retirement funds (4%) as an income source.

Figure 3: Source of income reported at application

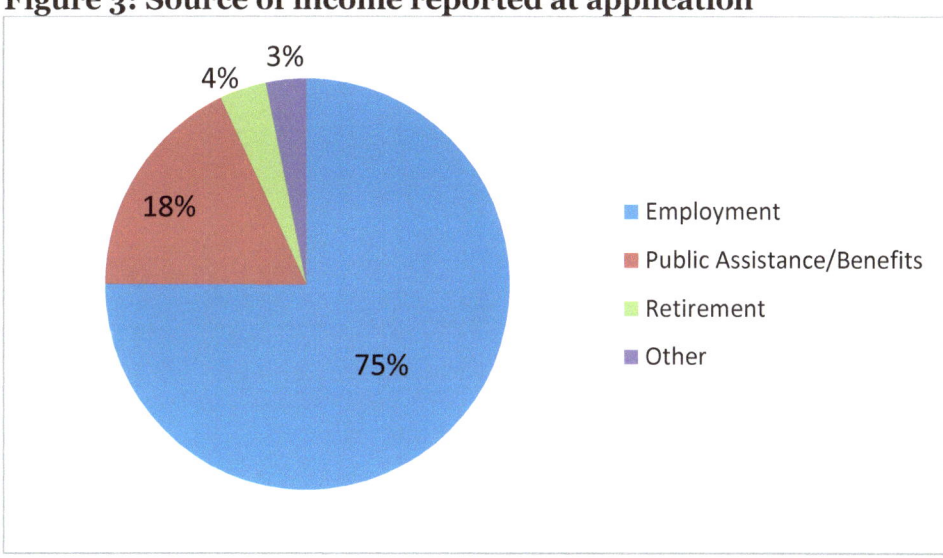

Reported government assistance or benefit income received by the consumers in our sample consists largely of Social Security payments (including Supplemental Security Income and Social Security Disability Insurance),[22] unemployment, and other federal or state public assistance.[23] These payments are usually of a fixed amount, typically occurring on a monthly basis. As shown in Figure 4 below, borrowers reporting public assistance or benefits as their income source are more highly concentrated towards the lower end of the income range for the payday borrowers in our sample.

---

[22] Supplemental Security Income (SSI) payments are to qualified adults and children with disabilities and people who are 65 years or older with limited income and resources. Social Security Disability Insurance payments are to persons with disabilities who have paid enough employment taxes to the Social Security Trust Fund.

[23] It is possible that some benefit payments from private sources such as employer-provided disability benefits may also be captured in this category.

Figure 4: Distribution of income reported at application by source

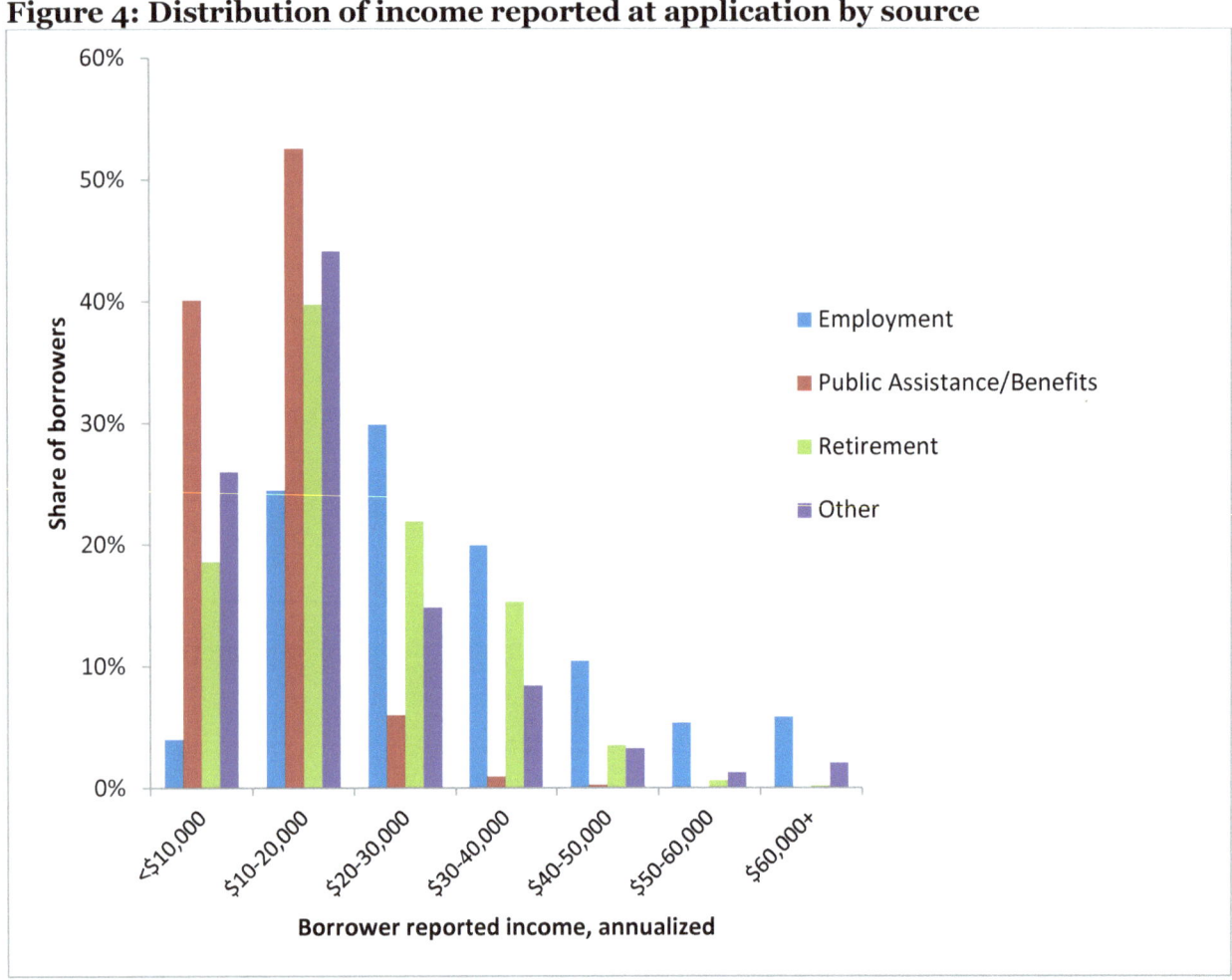

Note: Percentages represent share of borrowers in each income range within each income source category.

3.1.3 Intensity of Use

One of the primary goals of our analysis is to understand payday loan usage patterns. This section provides preliminary findings on the extent to which consumers in the study sample used this product during the 12-month study period and on the patterns of that use.[24] In order

---

[24] Loan usage patterns are based on our sample borrowers who take out a loan in the initial month of a lender's dataset. Usage is then tracked for a total of 12 months. These results thus reflect the subsequent experiences of a representative set of consumers whose loan usage would include the first month of the study sample. Therefore, our analysis does not reflect a given lender's portfolio over the course of a calendar year, since the lender would also have

to report usage levels consistently across borrowers, we consider loans and any rollovers of existing loans as separate transactions. For example, a consumer who takes out one loan and rolls it over once is considered to have two transactions (or loans) for purposes of this white paper. Similarly, a consumer who takes a loan, pays it back, and opens a new loan would also be considered to have two transactions.

Figure 5 below shows the distribution of loan use across consumers in our sample. Usage is concentrated among those consumers in our sample with 7 or more transactions in the 12-month study period. Nearly half (48%) of borrowers had more than 10 transactions over this same time period; of these, 29% (14% of all borrowers) had over 20 transactions. In contrast, 13% of borrowers had 1-2 transactions and another 20% had 3-6 transactions over the 12-month period. These consumers had a relatively low intensity of use.[25]

---

loan volumes and revenues derived from borrowers who do not take loans in the first month. Two factors may cause the usage statistics in our sample to show somewhat more intense usage than analyses based on all loans made in a calendar year. First, high-intensity borrowers are more likely to be sampled based on usage in a given month than low-intensity borrowers. Second, we exclude borrowers whose initial loan in the 12-month study period occurs after the initial month in the lender's sample, since their usage cannot be tracked over a full 12 months.

[25] Usage rates include borrowers who default and may become ineligible for future payday loans. For instance, some share of borrowers who take out a single payday loan may have this low amount of usage because they never paid their loan back and, as a result, were not provided additional credit by that lender in our 12-month study period.

Figure 5: Distribution of loan use, volume, and fees

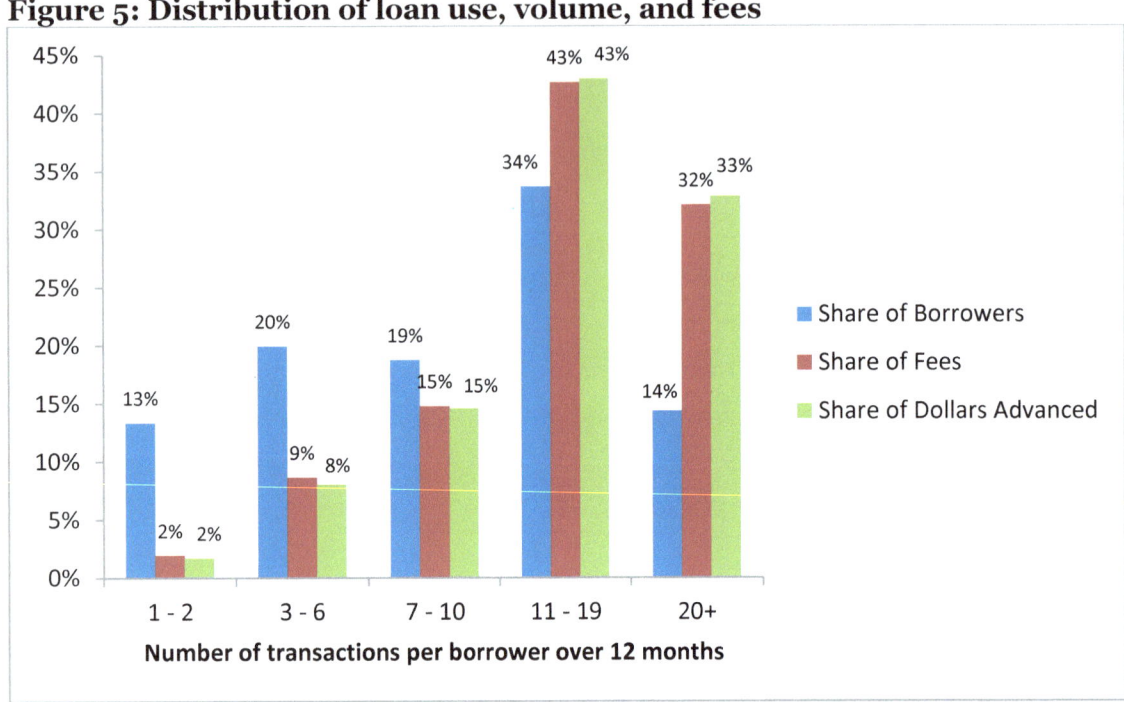

The figure also shows the distribution of loan volume and loan fees across consumer usage groups. Three-quarters of all loan fees generated by consumers in our sample come from those with more than 10 transactions during this period. In contrast, loan fees generated by consumers who borrowed six or fewer times over 12 months make up 11% of the total for this sample of borrowers.[26]

Overall, the median consumer in our sample conducted 10 transactions over the 12-month period and paid a total of $458 in fees, which do not include the loan principal.[27] One quarter of borrowers paid $781 or more in fees.

---

[26] As described in n. 24 above, these data differ from what would be observed in a lender's overall portfolio over a one-year period.

[27] An important policy question here is the benefit the consumer receives, in the form of credit extended, in return for the fees paid. As shown in Figure 6 in a subsequent section, many new loans are taken out within the same day a previous loan is repaid or shortly thereafter; therefore, it is arguable that these transactions should not be treated as new extensions of credit for this purpose.

Table 3: Number of transactions and total fees paid over 12 months

	# transactions	Total fees paid
Mean	10.7	$574
25th percentile	5	$199
Median	10	$458
75th percentile	14	$781

Since payday loans can be made for varying durations based on consumers' pay cycles, the frequency at which consumers received income may impact the number of transactions they conducted. Consumers paid on a more frequent basis may have the ability to take more loans over a certain period of time than others paid fewer times per year. The number of transactions conducted by a consumer can also be impacted by state law, which may cap the number of loans made in a given year or mandate cooling-off periods.[28] Because of this, we also examined the number of days in the 12-month study period that consumers were indebted. This provides a uniform measure for consumers with different use patterns, pay frequencies, and loan durations.

We find that consumers in our sample had a median level of 199 days indebted, or roughly 55% of the year. A quarter of consumers were indebted for 92 days or less over the 12-month study period, while another quarter was indebted for more than 300 days. The length of time a consumer is indebted is driven by three factors: (1) the number of transactions they conduct; (2) the number of days until each loan is due; and—to a much lesser extent—(3) whether that consumer has delinquent loans that remain outstanding beyond the contractual due date.

Table 4: Number of days and share of the year indebted

Mean	196	54%
25th percentile	92	25%
Median	199	55%
75th percentile	302	83%

---

[28] Some states have laws that would restrict maximum usage, such as an eight loan per year limit in Washington, a minimum loan duration of two pay cycles in Virginia, and mandated cooling-off periods after a certain amount of usage in Oklahoma and Virginia.

3.1.4 Sustained Use

Of particular importance to our analysis is the timing of the use of payday loans and whether we observe patterns of sustained, rather than sporadic, use. A pattern of sustained use may indicate that a borrower is using payday loans to deal with expenses that regularly outstrip their income. It also may indicate that the consumer is unable to pay back a loan and meet her other expenses that occur within the same pay period.

To shed light on this issue, we evaluate the distribution of borrowing patterns across consumer usage groups. This allows us to observe the share of transactions that are consistent with a pattern of sustained use, defined as transactions which occurred either the same day a previous loan was closed or soon after. Figure 6 below classifies consumers into five groups based on the number of transactions they conducted over the 12 month period. For each group, we can observe what share of transactions conducted by these consumers are the initial loans or loans after a break in indebtedness of at least 15 days. Likewise, we can observe the share of transactions that occurred shortly after a previous loan was closed—either the same day, within 1-7 days, or within 8-14 days.

Figure 6: Share of transactions initiated within 14 days of a previous transaction

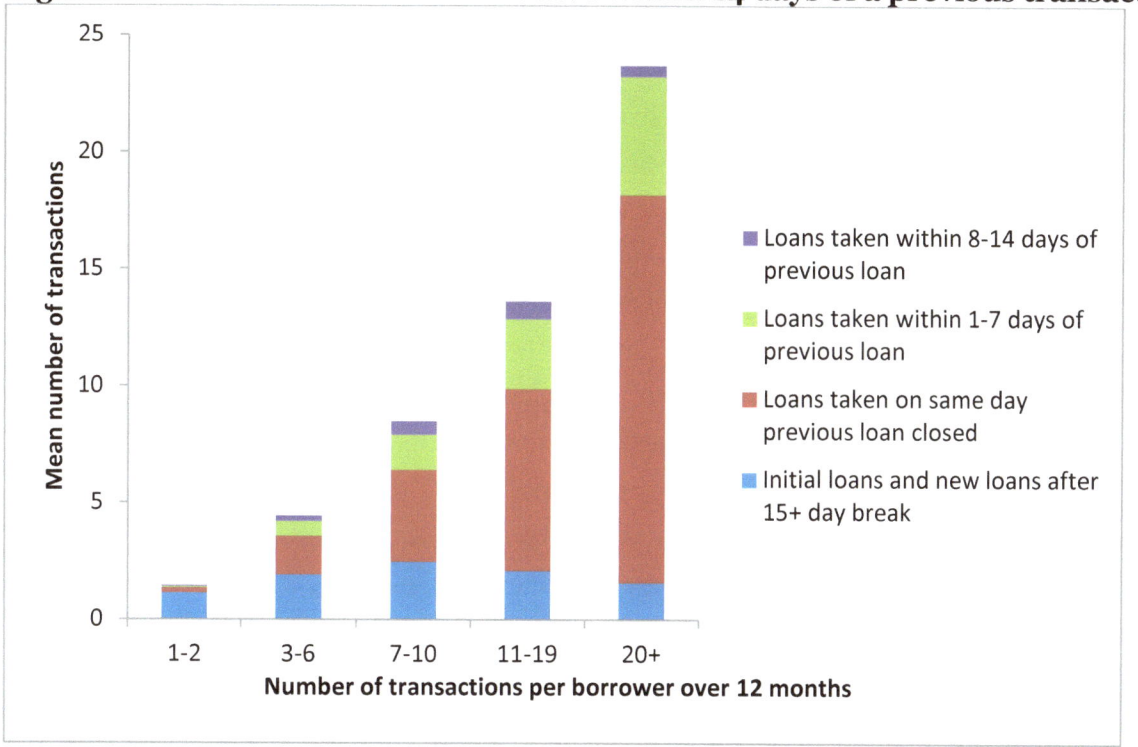

Note: The total height of each bar represents the mean number of transactions a borrower in each usage category conducted over 12 months. The height of each sub-category represents the mean number of transactions per consumer in the 12-month period that were conducted on the same day, within 1-7 days, or within 8-14 days of the close of a previous loan, as well as a sub-category that represents initial loans and new loans opened 15 days or longer after a previous loan was repaid.

The vast majority of loans made to consumers with 1-2 transactions in the 12 month period were either initial loans or loans taken after a 15 day or longer break. By definition, all borrowers with a single transaction would meet these criteria since they only took an initial loan.

For those consumers taking out more than two loans during the 12 month period, an increasing share were attributable to transactions that are taken out on a sustained basis; that is, within 14 days of the prior loan. Transactions taken by consumers with 3-6 loans in the 12 month period were about evenly split between continuous loans and loans that are either the initial in our study period or taken out after a 15 day or longer break after closing the previous loan.

The majority of transactions conducted by consumers with at least 7 transactions a year were taken on a nearly continuous basis. Most frequently, these new transactions were opened within a day of a previous loan closing. We discuss the significance of these findings in the final section of this paper.

3.2 Deposit Advances

For our study of deposit advances, we gathered data from a number of depository institutions. Some of these data are used here to describe outcomes for consumers during a 12 month study period. Since deposit advance eligibility typically depends on recent electronic deposit history, NSF and overdraft activity, and previous deposit advance use, a consumer's eligibility can fluctuate over time. Consumers included in this analysis had accounts that were either: (1) eligible to take an advance during the first month of the study period or (2) eligible during subsequent months if they had been eligible sometime during the quarter prior to the beginning of the study period.[29] Consumers with accounts opened after the beginning of the study period and accounts that became newly eligible later in the study period were excluded. Based on these criteria, an equal number of accounts were randomly selected for each institution; hence the outcomes reported here can be thought of as averages across institutions, rather than outcomes for the underlying population of accounts that satisfied these criteria.[30] This sampling methodology was used so that patterns measured below cannot be attributed to any specific institution.

About half of the institutions' consumer deposit accounts were eligible for deposit advances. Our sample contains more than 100,000 eligible accounts, with roughly 15% of accounts having at least one deposit advance during the study period. We compare deposit advance users and consumers who are eligible for—but did not take—any advances, as well as deposit advance users with varying levels of use.

---

[29] The data obtained by the CFPB covers a period longer than the study period and thereby enables us to observe eligibility prior to the start of the study period.

[30] The analysis of the deposit advance product presented in this paper draws on information collected through the supervisory process, aggregated to preserve the confidentiality of individual institutions.

3.2.1 Loan Characteristics

The median size of an individual advance was $180. However, consumers can take out multiple advances in small increments up to their specified credit limit prior to repaying outstanding advances and associated fees out of the next electronic deposit. Thus, merely observing the size of an individual advance without considering the number of advances taken before repayment may not fully capture the extent of borrowing.

To provide a more meaningful representation of loan characteristics, we also analyzed each "advance balance episode," defined as the number of consecutive days during which a consumer has an outstanding deposit advance balance. The median average daily balance of all advance balance episodes was $343, which is larger than the $180 median advance. This reflects the tendency of some consumers to take multiple advances prior to repayment.

To measure the duration and APRs associated with incremental deposit advance use or repayments from multiple deposits, we again used the concept of advance balance episodes. Each advance balance episode has a well-defined duration and average daily outstanding balance that can be used to measure an APR, given total advance fees that are a fixed percent of advances extended during the period.[31]

We took this approach to measuring APRs in dealing with consumers who take incremental advances prior to the receipt of the next electronic deposit and with advances that are repaid out of successive electronic deposits credited to the account at different dates. When a consumer takes multiple advances prior to a given incoming electronic deposit, each is subject to the same fee measured as a percent of the advance amount. However, each advance will have a different duration (measured as the number of days until repayment) and, therefore, a different APR. Similarly, when an incoming electronic deposit is insufficient to fully repay an outstanding deposit advance balance, segments of the advance repaid at a different dates will have varying durations (and, again, different APRs).

---

[31] This fee-based APR calculation is solely intended to facilitate comparisons between payday loans and deposit advances for the purposes of this white paper and should not be relied upon for any other purpose. When disclosing APR, lenders must comply with currently applicable legal requirements.

The median duration of advance balance episodes in our sample was 12 days. Using this duration, we can calculate an APR for different fees that may be charged for an advance. For example, a typical fee is $10 per $100 borrowed.[32] This fee would imply an APR of 304% given a 12-day duration. A hypothetical lower fee of $5 per $100 advanced would yield an APR of 152%, while a hypothetical higher fee of $15 per $100 advanced and would yield an APR of 456% with the same 12-day term. Thus, the APR will vary significantly depending on the duration of a particular advance balance episode and the fee charged by an individual institution.

3.2.2 Consumer Account Characteristics

While we did not directly observe the total income of consumers who use deposit advances in our sample, we did observe deposits to their accounts. We can also measure other account characteristics in our data, such as average daily balances, and how consumers transact from their accounts. An important part of our analysis was to compare how these types of account activity differ for consumers who use advances and for consumers who are eligible for deposit advances but do not use the product ("eligible non-users"). In general, these findings are measured on an average per-month basis for the months that the deposit account was open during the study period.

Consumers in our study sample who took deposit advances had a median of just under $3,000 in average monthly deposits. While monthly deposits are not necessarily indicative of, or directly comparable to, monthly income (deposits can reflect money transferred into an account from other sources), average monthly deposits do reflect available resources. As compared to eligible non-users, consumers taking deposit advances tended to have slightly lower average monthly deposits.

---

[32] This fee is expressed in slightly different ways depending on the institution, such as $2 per $20 borrowed, or $1 per $10 advanced, but is the equivalent to a $10 fee for every $100 borrowed.

Figure 7: Average monthly deposits

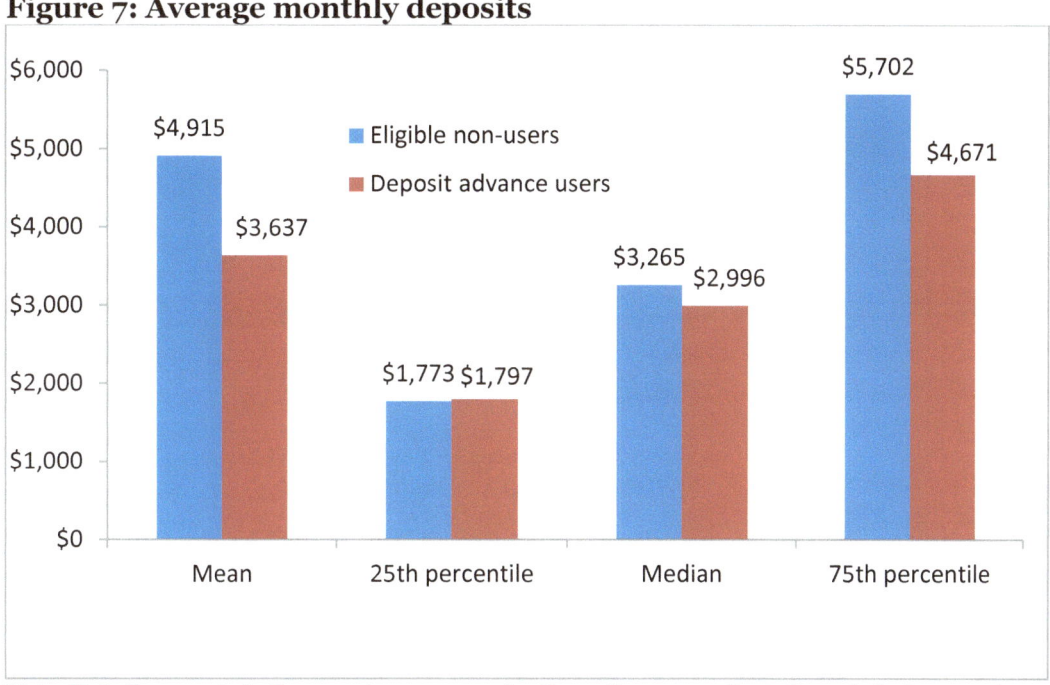

Note: Not all accounts in the sample were open for the entire 12-month study period. Average deposits were measured for months during which the account was open.

Consistent with lower deposits to the account, deposit advance users also tended to have a lower volume of payments and other account withdrawals than eligible non-users.

Figure 8: Average monthly consumer-initiated debits

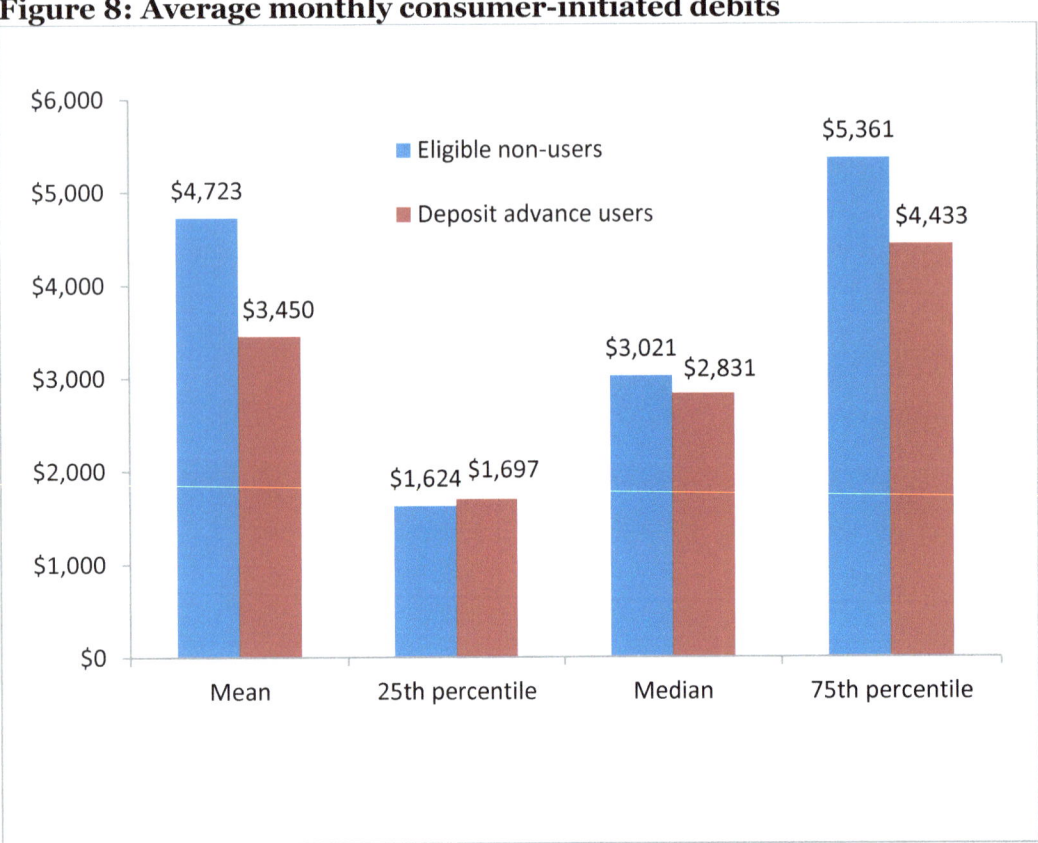

Note: Not all accounts in the sample were open for the entire 12-month study period. The average dollar volume of consumer-initiated debits was measured for months during which the account was open.

However, deposit advance users tended to conduct a larger number of account transactions than eligible non-users, particularly debit card transactions.

Figure 9: Average monthly number of consumer-initiated debits

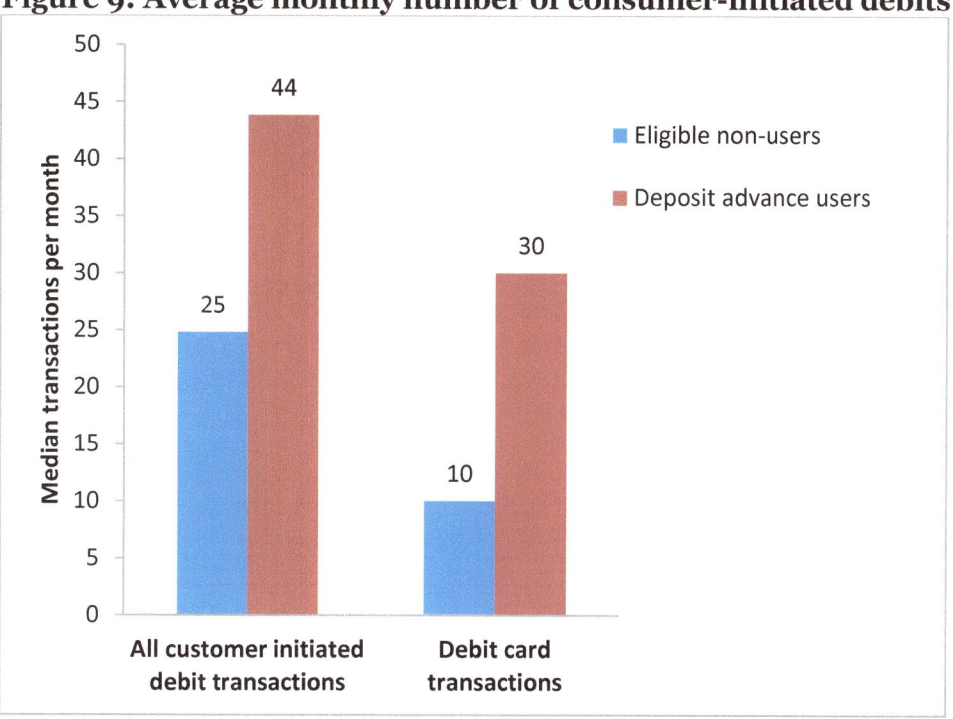

Note: Not all accounts in the sample were open for the entire 12-month study period. The average number of consumer-initiated debits per month is measured for months during which the account was open.

Deposit advance users tended to have much lower average daily balances than eligible non-users. This suggests that deposit advance users have less of a buffer to deal with financial short-falls (balances reported here include deposit advances that have been credited to a consumer's deposit account).

Figure 10: Average daily account balance

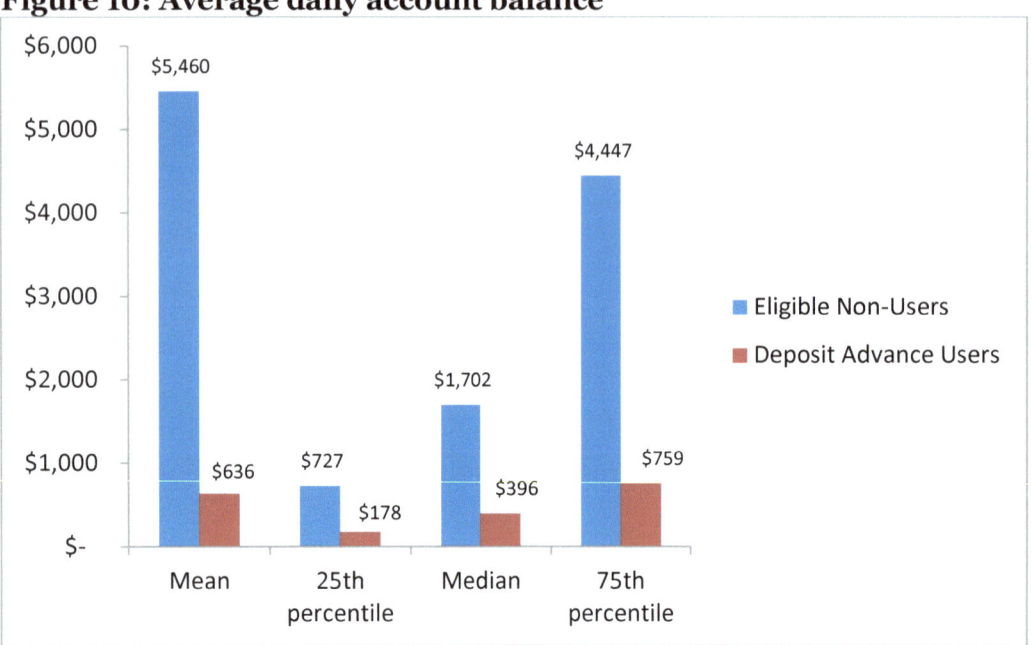

Note: Not all accounts in the sample were open for the entire 12-month study period. The average daily account balance for each account is measured for days during which the account was open.

3.2.3 Intensity of Use

To better understand how consumers in our sample use deposit advances, we first present information on the number of advances taken and total dollar amount advanced during the study period, as well as the number of advance balance episodes deposit advance users have over the 12-month study period.

As previously explained, because consumers can take multiple advances up to their specified credit limit with repayment out of the next electronic deposit, measuring the number of advances is not necessarily an accurate means of measuring the intensity of use. For example, a consumer who takes out two advances each of $50 on successive days is not necessarily using the product more intensely than a consumer who takes out a single advance of $100. To assess intensity of use in light of the incremental nature of some consumers' use of the deposit advance product, we classify accounts in terms of the total dollar volume of advances taken during the 12-month study period rather than the number of advances that were extended.

As with payday borrowers, we found that a significant share of deposit advance borrowers took a sizable volume of advances during the 12-month study period. On the one hand, 30% of all borrowers in our sample had total advances of no more than $1,500; which we refer to as light to moderate annual use of the deposit advance product. On the other hand, more than half of deposit advance users in our sample took advances totaling more than $3,000. Further, more than a quarter (27%) of deposit advance borrowers took advances totaling more than $6,000 over 12 months, and more than half of this group (14% of the total population of deposit advance borrowers) took advances in excess of $9,000.

The two highest usage groups accounted for 64% of the total dollar volume of advances and more than half (55%) of the total number of advances extended. In contrast, the borrowers who used $1,500 or less in advances during the same time period accounted for less than 10% of the total dollar amount and number of advances.

Figure 11: Distribution of loan use and volume

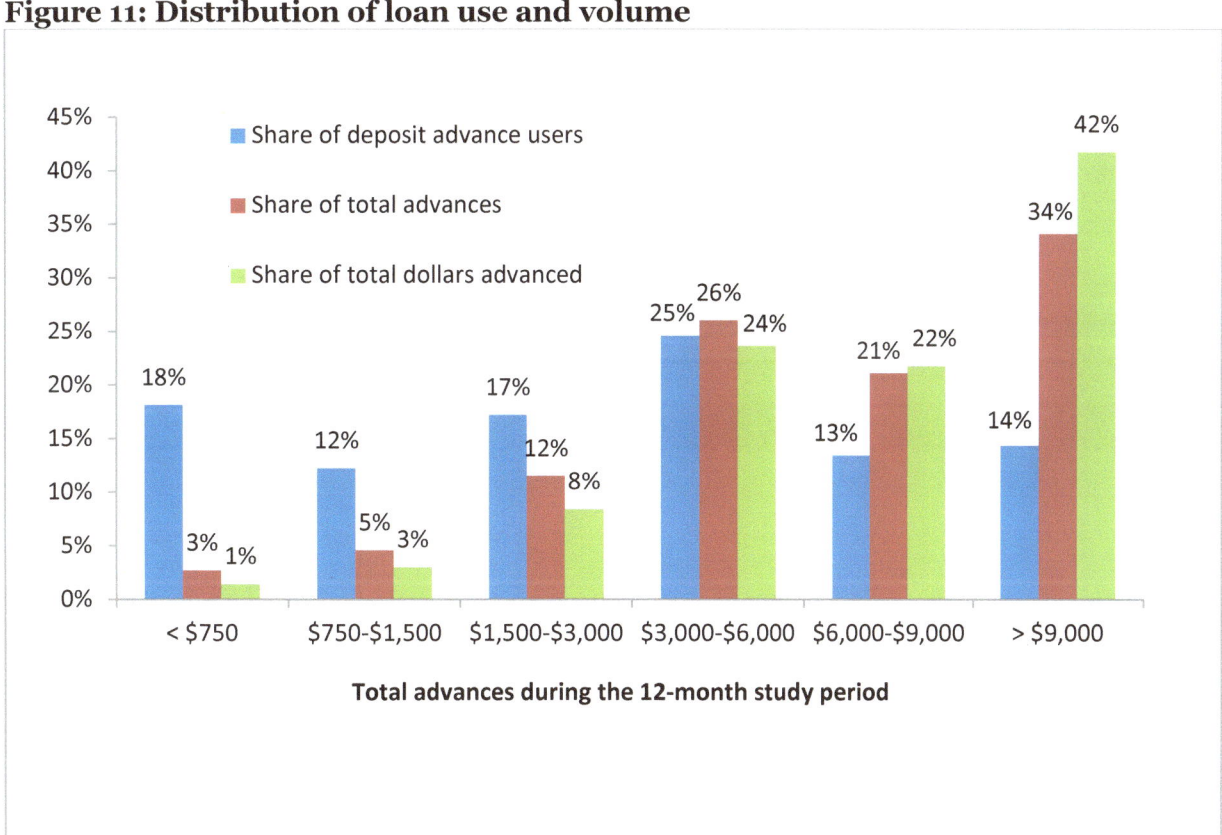

Note: Each account is classified by the dollar volume of deposit advances taken during the 12-month study period. Not all accounts in the sample were open for the entire study period.

Table 5 illustrates that higher deposit advance usage during the 12-month period tends to reflect borrowers' frequent, as well as larger, advances.

Table 5: Median amount per advance and median number of advances

| | All account with advances | Amount use groups | | | | | |
		<$750	$750-$1,500	$1,500-$3,000	$3,000-$6,000	$6,000-$9,000	>$9,000
Median amount per advance	$180	$100	$100	$100	$160	$200	$200
Median number of advances	14	2	6	11	17	26	38

Note: Each account was classified by the dollar volume of deposit advances taken during the 12-month study period. Not all accounts in the sample were open for the entire study period.

As discussed in a previous section, we also measure use in terms of each advance balance episode—defined as the period of time in which a consumer has an advance outstanding. We found that the median number of episodes for all advance users in our study sample is eight per year. This varied from a median of just two episodes for the lowest use group to a median of 19 episodes for the highest use group.

Figure 12: Median number of advance balance episodes over 12-month period

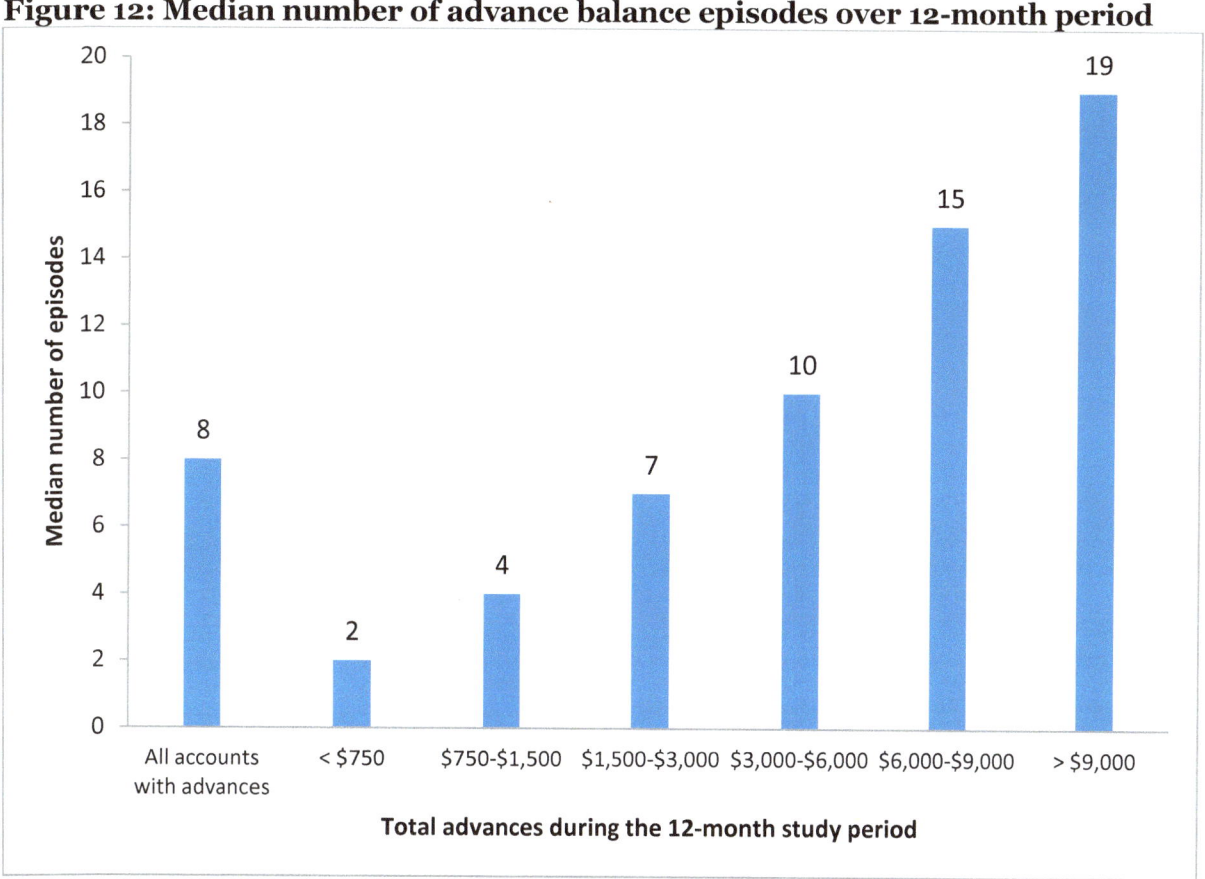

Note: An advance balance episode is defined as a period during which the account holder had an outstanding deposit advance balance. An advance balance episode may involve more than one advance or more than one repayment. Not all accounts in the sample were open for the entire 12-month study period.

Higher usage during the 12-month study period also reflected larger outstanding balances during advance balance episodes. For the lowest usage group, the median average daily advance balance was $150, while for consumers in the two highest usage groups, average daily balances of advance balance episodes tended to exceed $400.

Figure 13: Average outstanding advance balance

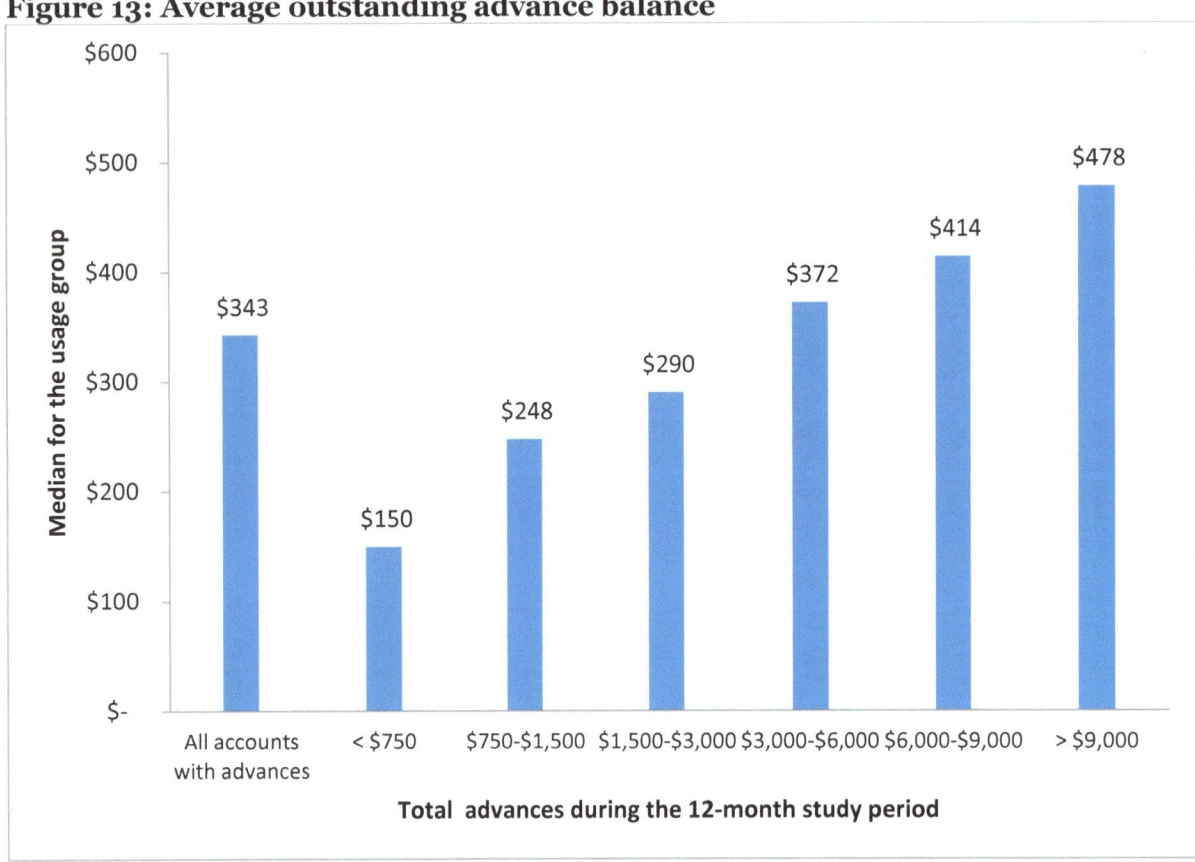

Note: An average daily balance is computed for each period during which an account holder has an outstanding deposit advance balance. Not all accounts in the sample were open for the entire 12-month study period.

We also measured the total number of days that each consumer in our sample was indebted by using the duration of each advance balance episode. Consumers in our sample were indebted for a median of 112 days (31% of the year), with the number of days generally increasing with the total volume of advances taken. Consumers taking more than $3,000 in advances during the 12-month study period tended to be indebted for more than 40 percent of the year.

Figure 14: Median total days with outstanding advance balance

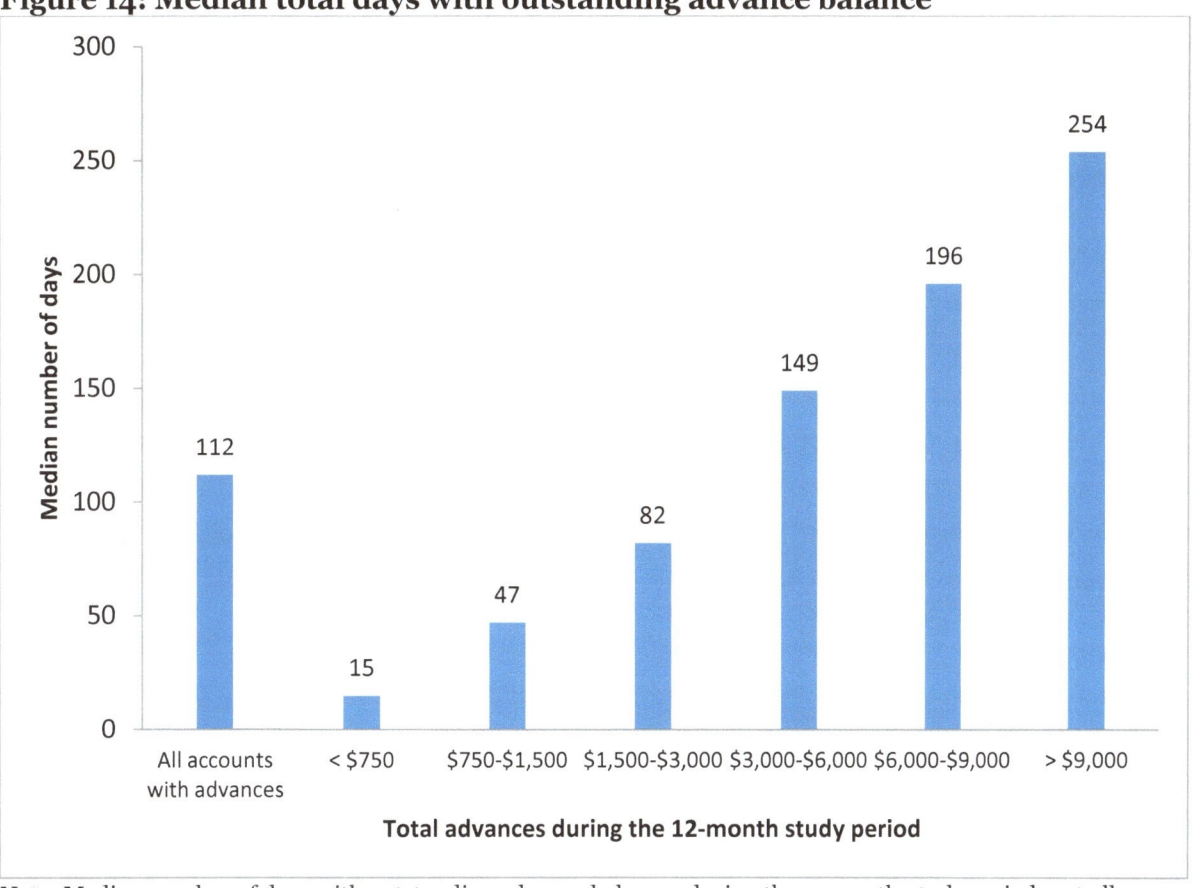

Note: Median number of days with outstanding advance balances during the 12 month-study period; not all accounts in the sample were open for the entire 12-month study period.

It is important to note that because we are analyzing consumers based on their eligibility for the deposit advance product, reported usage patterns are not directly comparable to those analyzed for payday borrowers that were included in the sample only if they had taken a loan in the first month of the study period. The deposit advance usage patterns measure usage by consumers who were eligible to use the product at the beginning of the sample period, but some consumers who used the product may not have done so until later in the year. Neither the payday loan nor the deposit advance findings capture any continuing use after the 12-month period analyzed. Usage patterns for both products also reflect use that ends because a consumer does not repay the loan and hence, the account is charged off.

3.2.4 Sustained Use

In addition to examining the advance activity of consumers during the 12-month period, we also analyze whether that indebtedness (measured in terms of advance balance episodes) occurred on a sustained, nearly uninterrupted basis.

We examined the total number of months in which each consumer in our sample took deposit advances and the longest number of consecutive months that advances were used. The median number of months in which a consumer had outstanding advance balances was seven; however consumers with $1,500 or less in annual advances typically had outstanding advances in four or fewer months while consumers with over $3,000 in annual advances typically had outstanding advances in 9 or more months, and at least six consecutive months during the 12-month period we examined here. It is important to note that that not all consumers were eligible to take deposit advances in every month of the study period so breaks in usage may be attributable to other factors.[33]

---

[33] For example, some accounts closed before the end of the study period. And, while most accounts were open for the entire period, many consumers were not eligible to take deposit advances for the entire year. In addition to other criteria that affect eligibility, variations also reflect policies requiring cooling-off periods after a specific period and/or intensity of use. Cooling-off policies are reflected in a reduction in amount of time that heavy advance users are eligible during the 12-month study period, compared to otherwise similar consumers with less usage. As intended, cooling-off policies set an upper bound on the number of months consumers can take advances.

Figure 15: Months with deposit advance activity

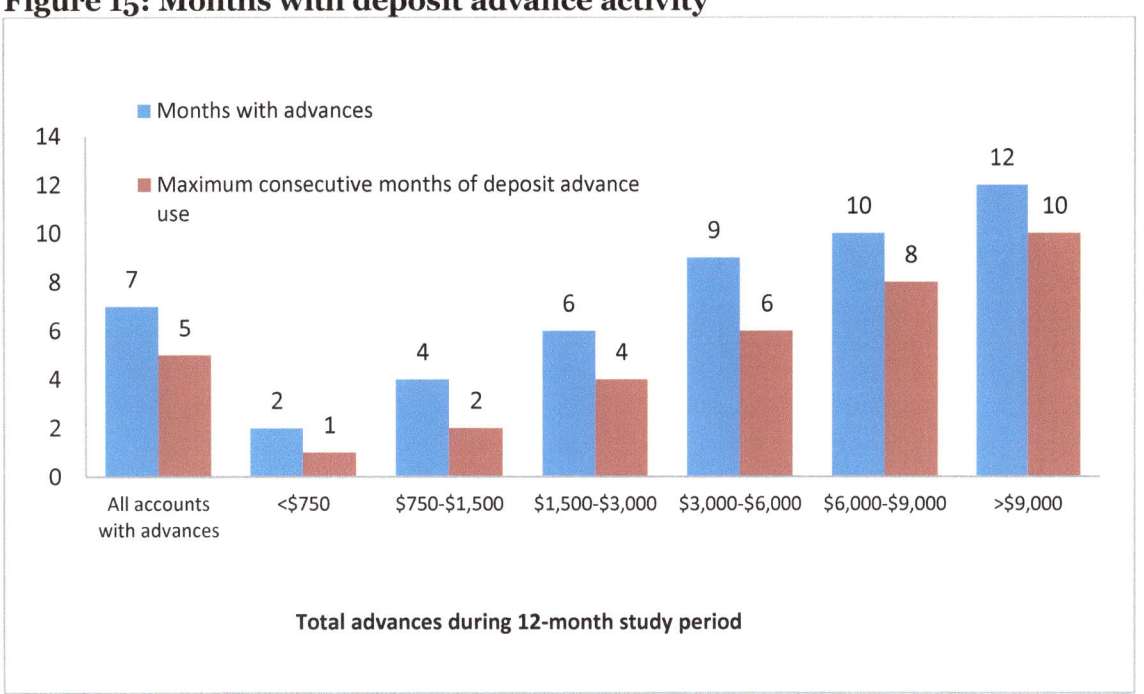

Note: Not all accounts in the sample were open for the entire 12-month study period.

Likewise, to determine whether advances are used with little break in between, we can observe the average number of days between each consumer's advance balance episodes using the dates that each deposit advance episode begins and ends.

Among consumers in our sample with more than one advance balance episode, the median number of days between advances was 13. Consumers who had the least use also had longer breaks between usage; for example, those consumers in the lowest usage group who had more than one advance episode had a median of 48 days between these uses of deposit advance. This break declined markedly among consumers with higher levels of use. Borrowers in the highest three usage groups tended to have 12 or fewer days between advance balance episodes.

Figure 16: Average number of days between advance balance episodes

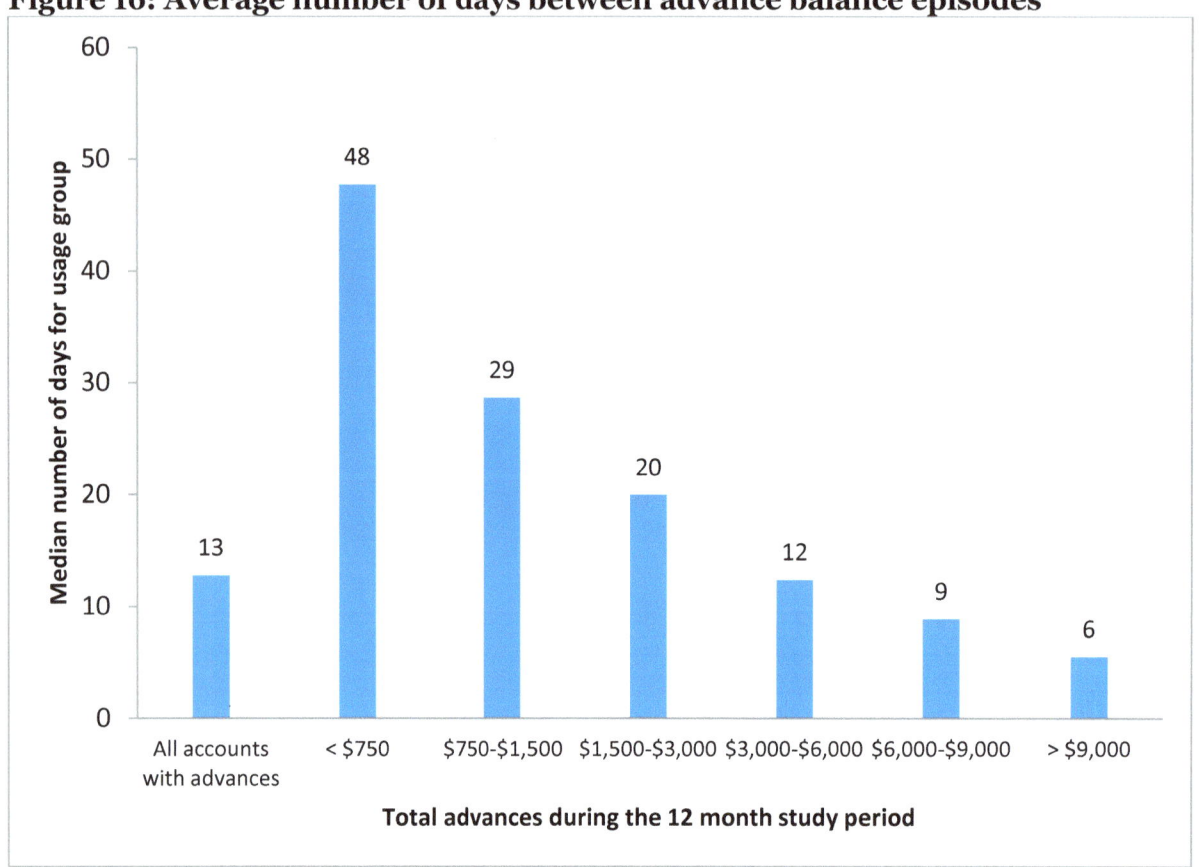

Note: The average number of days between a consumer's advances is calculated for each account with at least two advances during the 12-month study period; not all accounts in the sample were open for the entire 12-month study period.

3.2.5 Deposit Advance Use and Overdraft/NSF Activity

In addition to offering deposit advance, the depository institutions in our analysis may also provide overdraft coverage. Overdraft fees may be assessed when a depository institution pays items even though the consumer does not have sufficient funds in her account (or in another account which the consumer has linked to the deposit account). If, instead of paying the item, the bank elects to return it as an unpaid NSF item, a fee may also be charged.

Some institutions market deposit advances as a way for consumers to avoid overdraft fees when they do not have sufficient funds in their accounts to cover transactions. However, deposit advances are typically not offered as a form of "overdraft protection" that would automatically cover non-sufficient funds items up to a consumer's deposit advance limit. A consumer taking a deposit advance to add funds to her account balance must estimate the amount of funds needed to cover transactions that have not yet cleared as well as future transactions that will occur before the next deposit.

We found that deposit advance users in our sample of accounts were much more likely to have incurred an overdraft or NSF fee during the 12-month study period than eligible non-users. Notably, we found that while just 14% of eligible non-users incurred an overdraft or NSF fee during the 12 month study period, 65% of those consumers who used deposit advances had overdraft or NSF activity. Deposit advance users who incurred an overdraft or NSF fee typically incurred a greater number of fees than eligible non-users with at least one overdraft or NSF fee.

Figure 17: Overdraft and NSF Activity during the 12- month study period

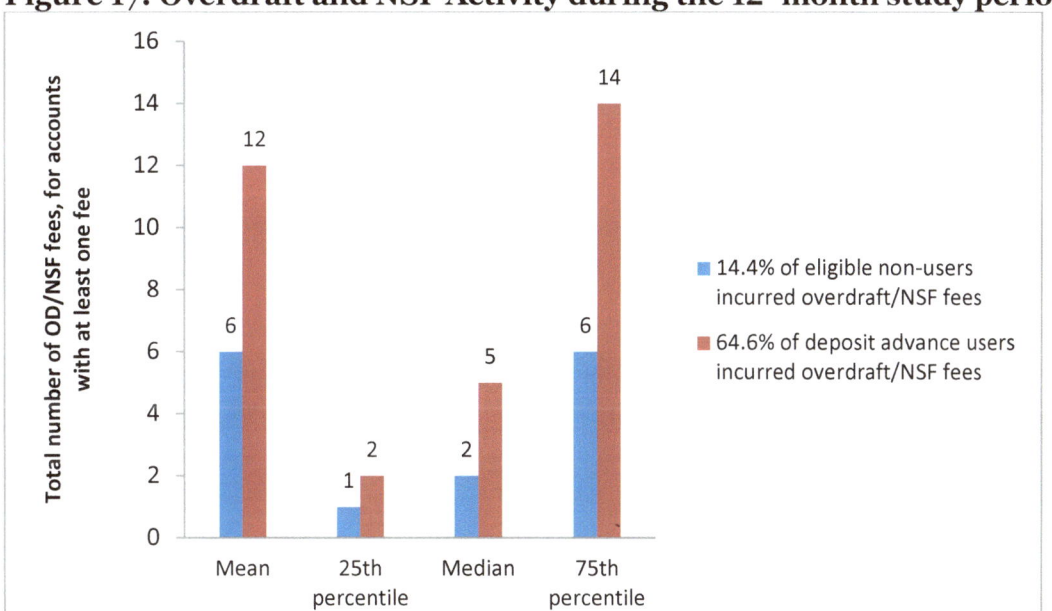

Note: For each account with at least one NSF or overdraft fee, total fees reflect all overdraft and NSF fees incurred by the account during the study period. However, not all accounts in the sample were open for the entire 12-month study period.

Consumers with greater deposit advance usage during the study period were more likely to have had overdraft or NSF transactions. Over four out of five consumers in the two highest usage groups had at least one overdraft or NSF.

Table 6: Deposit advance usage and overdraft/NSF fees during the 12 month-study period

		<$750	$750-$1,500	$1,500-$3,000	$3,000-$6,000	$6,000-$9,000	>$9,000
Accounts in deposit advance usage group with OD/NSF fees		45%	57%	63%	71%	82%	83%
Number of OD/NSF fees for accounts in usage group with any OD/NSF fees	Mean	7	9	10	13	17	16
	25th percentile	1	2	2	2	3	3
	Median	3	4	4	5	7	7
	75th percentile	7	9	11	14	19	18

Note: For each account with at least one overdraft or NSF fee, total fees reflect all overdraft and NSF fees incurred by the account during the study period. However, not all accounts in the sample were open for the entire 12-month study period.

Among consumers with overdraft or NSF activity, the total number of these items tended to increase with deposit advance usage. Among the four-fifths of consumers in the two highest usage groups with overdraft or NSF items, the median number of items was seven. However, a quarter of deposit advance users in our sample in the two highest usage groups with overdraft or NSF items had 18 or more.

4. Conclusions and Implications

Payday loans and deposit advances are both structured as products designed to meet short-term credit needs, with the full amount borrowed due at the next payday in the case of payday loans and due as soon as sufficient qualifying electronic deposits are received (but no later than 35 days) in the case of deposit advances.

It appears these products may work for some consumers for whom an expense needs to be deferred for a short period of time. The key for the product to work as structured, however, is a sufficient cash flow which can be used to retire the debt within a short period of time.

The data presented in this study suggest some consumers use payday loans and deposit advances at relatively low to moderate levels. Thirteen percent of payday borrowers in our sample took out only 1-2 loans over the 12-month period, and about one-third took out six loans or less. A similar share of deposit advance users (30%) took no more than a total of $1,500 in advances over the same period of time.

However, these products may become harmful for consumers when they are used to make up for chronic cash flow shortages. We find that a sizable share of payday loan and deposit advance users conduct transactions on a long-term basis, suggesting that they are unable to fully repay the loan and pay other expenses without taking out a new loan shortly thereafter. Two-thirds of payday borrowers in our sample had 7 or more loans in a year. Most of the transactions conducted by consumers with 7 or more loans were taken within 14 days of a previous loan being paid back—frequently, the same day as a previous loan was repaid. Similarly, over half of deposit advance users in our sample took out advances totaling over $3,000. This group of deposit advance users tended to be indebted for over 40% of the year, with a median break between advance balance episodes of 12 days or less.

We did not analyze whether consumers who use these products more heavily turned to a payday loan or deposit advance initially because of an unexpected, emergency expense or because their regular obligations outstripped their income. Nor have we analyzed what other strategies a consumer might employ, other products she might use in lieu of a payday loan or deposit advance, or the possible consequences or trade-offs associated with these choices. What appears clear, however, is that many consumers are unable to repay their loan in full and still meet their other expenses. Thus, they continually re-borrow and incur significant expense to repeatedly carry this debt from pay period to pay period. For both products, the high cost of the loan or advance may itself contribute to the chronic difficulty such consumers face in retiring the debt.

It is unclear whether consumers understand the costs, benefits, and risks of using these products. On their face, these products may appear simple, with a set fee and quick availability. However, the fact that deposit advances do not have a repayment date but rather are repaid as soon as qualified deposits are received adds a layer of complexity to that product which consumers may not effectively grasp. Moreover, consumers may not appreciate the substantial probability of being indebted for longer than anticipated and the costs of such sustained use. To the extent these products are marketed as a short-term obligation, some consumers may misunderstand the costs and risks, particularly those associated with repeated borrowing.

In addition, the current repayment structure of payday loans and deposit advances, coupled with the absence of significant underwriting, likely contributes to the risk that some borrowers will find themselves caught in a cycle of high-cost borrowing over an extended period of time. As we have seen, payday loans are generally required to be repaid at the consumer's next payday and deposit advances are repaid out of ensuing electronic deposits, typically derived from wages or other regular source of income. These products are represented as being appropriate for consumers who (1) have an immediate expense that needs to be deferred for a short period of time and (2) will have a sufficient influx of cash by the next pay period to retire the debt – and to pay the significant borrowing costs. Yet, it does not appear that lenders attempt to determine whether a borrower meets this profile before extending a loan. Lenders may instead rely on their relative priority position in the repayment hierarchy to extend credit without regard to whether the consumer can afford the loan. This position, in turn, trumps the consumer's ability to organize and prioritize payment of debts and other expenses. Other structural and usage characteristics may also play a material role in harms experienced by consumers.

Our findings thus raise substantial consumer protection concerns. The CFPB intends to continue its inquiry into small dollar lending products to better understand the factors contributing to the sustained use of these products by many consumers and the light to moderate use by others. We will analyze the effectiveness of limitations, such as cooling-off periods, in curbing sustained use and other harms. Separately, we are analyzing borrowing activity by consumers using online payday loans.

The CFPB recognizes its responsibility to implement Federal consumer financial laws to ensure that "markets for consumer financial products and services are fair, transparent and competitive." The CFPB is also authorized to "prescribe rules ... identifying as unlawful unfair, deceptive or abusive acts or practices in connection with ... the offering of a consumer financial product or service" (among other rulemaking authority) and to act to prevent covered persons or service providers (as defined in title X of the Dodd-Frank Wall Street Reform and Consumer Protection Act) "from committing or engaging in" such acts or practices.[34] The potential consumer harm and the data gathered to date are persuasive that further attention is warranted to protect consumers. Based upon the facts uncovered through our ongoing work in this area, the CFPB expects to use its authorities to provide such protections.

---

[34] Dodd-Frank Wall Street Reform and Consumer Protection Act, Pub. L. No. 111-203, tit. X, 124 Stat. 1376 (2010). See sections 1021(a), 1031(a), and 1031(b).